ISBN 0-9665478-1-0

Edited by Fred Burwell and Mary Hughes-Greer
Design and Layout by Jeremy Saperstein
Printed by BookMasters, Inc.
All photos courtesy of JoAnne McFarland

Address all correspondence to:
Acorn Whistle Press
907 Brewster Avenue
Beloit WI 53511

First Edition

ACKNOWLEDGEMENTS

The author gratefully acknowledges the following journals in which earlier versions of these poems appear:

Incident and **Where We Begin** *African-American Review* (Summer 1996).

Sisters, **Time To Lose** and **Sanctum** *Obsidian II: Black Literature in Review* (Spring - Summer 1996).

In The Groove, **Three Deep Spaces**, **Reveille** and **Missing Person** *Acorn Whistle* (Volume 2, Number 2 – Spring 1998).

Johnnycake, **Diversion** and **Journey** *Acorn Whistle* (Volume 3, Number 1 – Spring 1999).

Directions *Great Midwestern Quarterly* (Summer 1999).

The author would also like to thank:

Kevin Thomas for the wellspring of his love which makes everything possible.

Editors — Fred Burwell and Mary Hughes-Greer for their unstinting generosity with time and expertise.

The eight wisewriters: Gretta Sabinson, Anne Adams-Lang, Marilyn Kaye, Katherine Leiner, Michele Willens, Bette Glenn, Lavinia Plonka and Jane Furse for making sure the right words were in the right place.

Mia Brandt, Gail Benjamin and Phyllis Wrynn for their enthusiasm and benevolent insights.

Stephen and Elisabeth Thomas for the light they bring to every one of my days.

For my mother

CONTENTS

IN CAMERA

Sisters...8
Sanctum...10
Clan...11
Dorothy...12
Three Deep Spaces..13
Time to Lose...14
In Bed...15
Accident..16

EXPOSURES

Where We Begin..18
Johnny..19
Stain..20
Elvis and Me...22
Journey...24
Contrast..25
July 4th 1965..26
Diversion...27
Ashes to Ashes...28
Evening in Paris..29
Mr. Softie..30
In the Groove..31
Directions..33
Daddy's Girl..34
Missing Person..35
Skill...37

SOUNDVIEW

A Lot..40
Glo...42
Midsummer Night..43
Beauty Is...44
Johnnycake..45
Reveille..46
Patent Leather..47
Jacks...48
Mrs. Velasquez...49
Ordained..50
Aunt Ivy's..51
Icy Way..53
The Tent...54
Vision..55
This Old Heart of Mine..............................56
First Boy...57

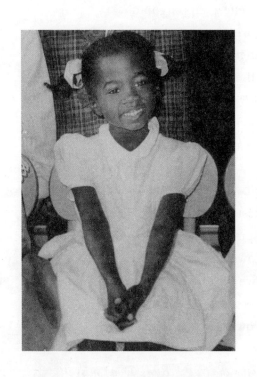

IN CAMERA

SISTERS

Coouuusin Bruucciie!!! WABC!
And so we begin/ rising to the sound of The Supremes and
The Marvelettes/ slipping into
summer's dress/ racing down the dim
piss-smelling stairway 26
steps into the sunkiss of July/ rolling on our
backs in the grass/ skin hot as the cement walk/ shiny
black as the ribbon of street
   See the auburn highlights in our
top hairs?   Swimming in the babel of a thousand
outside voices/ we watch the boys stripped
to their waists/ wrestle the wildcat water of the
hydrant/ spraying the people on the 27
bus/ windows open/ everyone wet   Midday
MOMmy! we scream
we track her arm out our third
floor window/ 50¢ tied in the end of a hanky   We snap
it up
     Don't miss the truck! Run! Don't miss it!
The whip-crack of our rope as we play
double dutch/ legs pumping/ flashes
of panties white as the rim of a colt's eye   9PM
Breaking out the anonymous embrace of the street/ the
freedom of being everyone's child/ upstairs
slow/ cradling the Thom
McAn box of grass and stones collected by the
river/ in the sink the whole day's dirt streaking

the soap/ the prize
of sleep/ the dark belly of a moon-kissed
August night/ sweet sucking humid   We are
two girls catty-cornered in a back room/ wrapped in the pristine
shroud of our sheets/ watching our walls
shimmering lavender

SANCTUM

The inside of our house was a female place/ a womb of
rooms where we placed our favorite objects
center stage/ vibrant accents that glowed like the blue
witch ball Tania gave me one birthday that sat on the dresser
for years/ its translucent
power/ the beacon I rose by each day

Summers/ all the windows opened wide
let out the stale heat/ let new
heat in/ lying on the couch in the dark
passing ice cubes wrapped in
dish towels up and down
our thighs/ mixing water with sweat/ naked
before the cyclops eye of
the television

Winters/ hiding under the bed/ finding
objects we'd lost months before layered with dust/ tight
in pockets next to walls painted hospital
green/ our mouths near the gaping hole of the radiator pipe that
passed from apartment to apartment/ 7 floors
talking to the kids who lived below us late one night
six mouths warmed by the hot pipe
filling the space with voices intimate as lovers/ the radio
playing in the background   6AM Lying in the
halflight of dawn/ overcome by
sleep/ the air in the room like
blue smoke/ charged with the musky perfume of
our cabala

CLAN

Within moments of sitting at the table the matches
flare/ in the air the bitter tang of
phosphorus/ the ashtray in the center of the table/ a pyre of
matches contorted as dried twigs/ the smoke
curling from the three cigarettes as if from man's
first fires/ and they
    my uncle my aunt my mother are a
tribe gathered for warmth under the night sky

As they talk funnels of smoke interlace over the
table/ mushrooming at the overhead light
one cigarette after the other/ a fellowship of
sparks as they marvel at my
fabulous father/ his escapades/ a child's latest
triumph

By midnight my mother's voice is
husky and broken/ Myrna's hawkish cough (the
cancer that came later) Lenny's eyes/ narrowed and
red/ they are dulled
sedated
    On the table
a mountain of tawny butts
rising from the ashes

Dorothy

Here I go
across Rosedale Avenue through the wrought iron gates of
The Academy Gardens/ eight
majestic buildings linked by a labyrinth of roads/ green as
Sherwood Forest/ twelve maples flanking
the main pass-through/ six other
ways in and out/ I could cut

four minutes off a trip to the butcher by
walking through/ instead of around
  A pound of chopped chuck please
or shave five minutes off a run to The Peppermint Bar for
Mommy's Marlboros/ inside dark
and cool as a cave/ the huge candy case right up front/ meticulous
rows of sugar daddies sugar babies kisses
candy necklaces lipsticks jawbreakers and the

fat man who crouched low on the stool behind/ thighs spread/ white
balloon hands tossing up sweets as I pointed them out/ laying down
my coins on the pimply rubber mat
Racing back through The Gardens cool foreign
the lush landscape of those with

more Pick
a road/ any road/ they all lead Home

THREE DEEP SPACES

In our apartment there were three deep spaces
without doors/ closets that never closed   We hung
curtains to mask what was behind/
towels and unpressed clothes/ high heels stacked in hills of
cardboard boxes/ puffy skirts and three inch patent
leather belts/ striped hatboxes from
Bonwit's/ button tins/ suitcases stuffed
with old letters/ boxes of photographs tied
with string/ a broken picnic basket
Some years
the curtains were wildly colored/ a sixties orgy of
hot pinks and lime/ other years a subdued olive or rose
without pattern   We'd sew them up
on the Singer when we wanted a change

We'd play hide and seek while
the adults smoked in the kitchen/ race like wild things
room to room/ squeezing into the black worlds behind the curtains
pressing our bodies (sometimes two or three) against the
volume of skirts/ giggling as we awakened the acrid
earth smell of
my mother/ the seductive odor of leather and sweat that
lined her shoes like a second sole   These were the first

best places to run/ our jewel hearts
pounding/ as we waited/ aching
to be discovered

TIME TO LOSE

9PM   I sit on the sidewalk
where the grass begins/ my arms over the low
chainlinks that don't KEEP us OFF THE GRASS/ pavement
warm as sun-baked cotton/ my baby
blue dress raised on my thighs/ the sky
open above me

Late water drips from the hydrant/ the bare boy who leans
to sip/ so dark he matches the evening/ the silver of his
buckle flashes/ his white sneakers and socks
comic in the growing night

As I lean back and swing on the chains
I listen to the percussive rasp of pebbles beneath my soles
The stars suspended over our piece of city
echo the rhythm that
throbs out the windows/ all the radios tuned to
the same beat/ the one I
swing to/ the hem of my dress sure as a
drummer's brush

In Bed

In bed our second life begins/ close heads
we croon *Moon*
River and *Downtown* 'til she screams *QUIET*
IN THERE!!   We giggle/ fiddling the covers with
hairless legs/ today you taught me how to shave/ and I
stroke silk skin twisting my calf in the laser
beam of light squeezing through the crack
dreaming a boyfriend's hand instead   You look sideways
whisper *Trent*/ kissed on the back stairs last week as I
watched/ jealousy a knotted fist in my stomach   I slide a
book from under my bed (seven
to return to the bookmobile
Friday) finish a chapter by
stolen light/ sleep sounds soft in your mouth/ your dark hand
splayed on the sheet —
a starfish

ACCIDENT

The day of the accident we were waiting for the train
on the elevated platform above Westchester
Avenue/ the avenue that never saw
sunlight/ except filtered
through the cracks of the tracks/ its abstract
fretwork on the cars below

We didn't see them run/ see the birth of the
thought/ the oldest's decision to risk it/ pulling his
sister by the hand   We only heard
impact/ heads jerked around/ the sound that registers
not in the rational mind but in the collective
unconscious/ the
wrong sound that means the
threat of death/ the tribe mobilized   Two children
down/ two of us watching from above/ the train coming in
fast/ our skirts inflated like lungs

EXPOSURES

Where We Begin

The bar is not crowded . . . few men . . . fewer women   Small
round tables/ metal legs like tuning forks/ tilt every
which way/ old chairs/ all black/ show pocked
pieces of wood

She was here once before/ this time a friend comes too
a weathercock

A manchild at the corner piano/ coppery
as a tobacco leaf/ pulling sweetness out of it like taffy/ his voice too
lyrics he's written himself/ his brown luster glance/ the pull
between her legs flowing out
concentric circles/ a stone dropped in a lake

Between sets they chat/ his eyes on her 24
karat smile/ her gift-wrapped legs that tug like
a fishing line/ her friend's eyes on
him

She scribbles her name and number inside a
matchbook/ he tosses it on the table as he turns to go/ tossing too
    I'll call

As she leaves she carries it back to him/ a talisman
and tucks it in his pocket/ her fingers brushing his
dark nipple/ hard as a
seed/ through the thin blue cloth
of his shirt

Johnny

He would bang on the door   as if to bring it down   his fists
mighty as the bad wolf's
breath   everything shaking   cursing at our
mother through the
steel between them   *Fe-Fi-Fo*
FUM!!   as his rage deepened and
spread   Lorna and I in the back bedroom
on our knees   the soft mattress
giving below us   close enough to feel each other's
heat

The night she
wouldn't let him in   he retreated
downstairs   and hurled obscenities at
all the open windows   giving up only

hours later   crawling to sleep under a
whispering tree   its branches spread over
his body like a
mantle

STAIN

Once Lorna said she saw Daddy with a gun
in the closet where we kept the coats
in the front near the door to
our apartment   The only way out

My mother's eyes bugged out
when she heard and she ran   She stopped
for her shoes but that's all
leaving five kids   her own two and three
others
        my cousin Lenny my cousin Leigh
my cousin Yvette   all
alone in the house   It was the first time
We hid behind our beds and waited   Lorna

laughed   that was her response to danger
we'd seen it before   the time she accidentally
set the fire on the stove   Lenny whimpered
I peed in my pants because the toilet was
too far but it would have happened anyway
because I wasn't thinking about my life
there in the room behind the bed —
behind my eyes I was fast-forwarding through
the awesome impossibility of our futures

I don't know what we were waiting for —
her to return or him to come and

kill us   one bullet for each   one saved
for himself
My mother came back using two officers as a block
They searched the apartment and found
my father in bed   got him up and asked him to explain
himself then
left   not having taken many notes   But Lorna still

swears she saw him and she struck a chord
in my mother   that invisible place in her mind where
the fact that my father might hate
himself enough to kill
her was mushrooming   like when the sperm
penetrates the egg and cells
start dividing   wildfire

Elvis and Me

I overheard when I was twenty-five
that the year my father wrote   *Stuck on You*
for Elvis Presley he made sixty thousand
dollars on that song alone   My uncle
said it to my mother but of course she already
knew that   it was just something they brought
out and examined now and then   close up
the way you might a beautiful
bug you came across on a stalk of grass as
you walked through a field of
millions

We saw none of it   He spent it on clothes
hotels his musician friends women-other-
than-my-mother alcohol and drugs   Or perhaps
he used it as a paper trail as he breasted the forests
of The Bronx to our house so he could find his way
out again   Or wiped himself with it then watched it
disappear down the hole and out to the river we
could see from our windows   By the time he got
to our door he was empty

It was when he died that we began to see the
money   And when Elvis died we began to see
more   our profits from their deaths
coming regular in lovely white envelopes
with windows so you could right away see the

money start   like you might see the promise of
snow out your window on a winter day   a third
for my mother   a third for my sister   a third for
me   (though she could have taken it all and we
wouldn't have blamed her)   Something we could
bank on   like Elvis could bet there would always be
black musicians who would feed him their songs
and he could use their sound to rise like
cream

Journey

We never saw him   the father without shoes
We slept through this story my mother tells
how he came home his brown feet
blackened   those feet she
insisted on loving   the man standing as if he
wore boots   filth
thicker than paint

Even the numbed woman was
stunned
   How did you get here?
The answer in his eyes that slid side to side in
unreason

That was the year we learned about the drinking gourd
the stars the slaves followed   the constellation that pulled
like a womb
to the north
the miles and miles and
miles they
braved   the threat of death
underfoot
their hearts in their

throats

CONTRAST

Out of morning's pale envelope slips
quiet
       We wake to find Daddy
at our table   He's come home to
remind us how bright he is
how dark we are

We blink in his raw light
listening with rapture
to the music of the teaspoon
that tests only the boundaries
of his coffee

JULY 4TH 1965

The day I let the firecrackers in the house
I carried them bold as the bouquets my father'd
brought us each that spring   asters for me
sweet williams for my sister   color-soaked
anemones for my mother   I'd
gotten them in the lot behind the building for
a few cents . . . contraband

It never occurred to me he would
set them off in the house   even after
the explosion and the acrid smell
of my mother's anger . . . everybody mad at me like
I did it   the four of us transfixed
by the stinking brown hole in the worn linoleum
Then she kicked us out and we
went to the movies   a double feature
He went off and left us   a garbled promise about
Later   We saw

Bye Bye Birdie and *The House of the Seven Gables*
and sandwiched between them I stood on the
slow-motion line for refreshments
the dark lobby thick with the heady fragrance
and   *chboot   chboot   chboot* of freshly
popping corn

DIVERSION

An April Saturday   fair weather   we play ball   the
    Spalding   makes continuous   parabolas
beneath our lifted legs
    'A' my name is Anna

Later   we link two
bobby pins for hopscotch   squares drawn in white chalk
the pavement almost dry   from yesterday's rain

Later still
I go to the Ruby's   buy a kite   some string   in the back
lot
we watch it   sail   pitch   dive   the river
below

    More string
we pull it up   the weedy grass
scratchy against our calves

When Daddy comes to get us
the kite glides past a   sliver of moon   he gives us change
for string   two balls more   and

we stay   our unfamiliar trio   in love   with the life on
the line   the kite   as it
strains towards the moon
    the only available light

Ashes to Ashes

There is only one light burning
the rest of the apartment is dark
From the couch I watch my father
doze in the lamp's unbroken circle of gold

On the table beside him   in the ashtray
his cigarette has burned to a
perfect cylinder of ash

I am waiting to see
who he will be when he
wakes up   when he notices the darkness   notices the day
extinguished

Only a few
latenight kids outside   singing
    Ring around the rosy
their circle undulating beneath the
blinding project lights

EVENING IN PARIS

Each year for Mother's Day we buy our
mother Evening in Paris
cologne
the festive window of the drugstore
lapis bottles showcased
up front   cutout hearts above
embossed   *MOM*
pink crepe paper streamers

Late nights our father phones
each of us on
an extension as he promises
     I will send you girls to college in
Europe . . . in Paris   his words
slurred   indistinct
                    only the word
Paris
distilled through the line   clean
and unadulterated   precious
as a pearl

MR. SOFTIE

Open the door and greet this
sober man
his eyes tapered porgies   the silvered whites
nutmeg-tinted irises   sunbursts
the shirt he's pressed himself
neat as an
origami carp   We ask him in
the kitchen cheery as a
party invitation
        He stays to dinner
his eyes traveling our faces   Outside
the late evening
ice cream truck   *Mister Softee*
wooing us with its lullaby

IN THE GROOVE

There was the day my father played
the 45 by Marvin Gaye   *Ain't That Peculiar*
in the living room 3 hours without
stopping   more tension in his body
than I'd ever seen   focusing like you would
on the last sound you would ever hear —
the last morsel of sweet food you would
take into your body and turn into
a little more life

I already knew the song by heart
We'd had the record for weeks and
we'd heard it on the radio months before that   I stood
in the passage from the hallway to the living room
unsure as always of the path between my father
and me   looking at the way he
wanted the music — the way you'd want milk for your baby
on the seventh day without
any   aching to have it to give
away as something he'd made —
like the way my mother made milk for Lorna and me
while she was sleeping walking making love
Magic she could do without even her mind on it

Even then I understood his rage
at the enormous effort of his life
to rise out of its own mute confusion

and form a pattern that would be
like what he was hearing — a beginning middle end
with a steady funky beat   lots of heat behind it
so smooth it sounded easy
as breathing

DIRECTIONS

Tonight the door is down and in he comes   not a stride of
victory but a stagger   my mother looks
daggers as she struggles to rein him in
But he wants
further in
and he's interrupted our baths   my sister invisible
behind the second door he would
force
her splashes stilled as she waits
(or is she stepping out and drying off?)
no lock
only my mother's might to
slow him
    No! she clips   he can't *see what he's made*   as I listen
shaking in our bedroom looking for something   anything
to kill

DADDY'S GIRL

One September afternoon he brought his cousin home
She was in from Chicago   That had never happened before
We'd seen no brothers no sisters no mother father
dead — as if he were his own
discrete creation

He carried a broken record player   two beer steins
in it   loose sheet music   We put the cousin in the
far chair and examined her   our teenage eyes unshy
searching for keys to our ancestry as our mother brought drinks
full of ice

She looked like him but as a woman —
his angles feminized   (but then I did too
everyone said so   lean nervous wiry radiating a high-strung
kinetic energy capped with lots of
hair)   He threw out   *Come*

sit on my lap! and patted it   (that was
new too) wanting to prove we could
fit together if we tried   but I felt awkward   sweating through the
thin pajamas I had not yet changed for
clothes   my new breasts firm as
kiwis   He laughed — a full thunderclap   tension
drenching everyone   the warmth of his legs
under mine
     unforgettable

Missing Person

It's the person who's missing who
claims the most attention   like when
a tooth is pulled from its
socket and the others can't help but
creep towards the space   jeopardizing their
own positions   the whole mouth
eventually losing its
integrity

One January morning on her way to work
my mother slipped and fell on the icy hill
outside our building   wrenching her ankle
badly   Later there was a bold ugly bruise
to be seen to   She thinks that's

when it happened   the killer cold finally
claiming my father   slumped in
tattered clothing over the grating caked
with ice   pinned like a butterfly
specimen   stone still   frozen
as if in a picture

Most likely it was a filthy hidden place
because no one found him for days
and when they did he was just another man
who'd irrevocably let himself
go   a john doe with a toe tag then

a beggar's plot in Queens
'til my mother's call to missing persons   owning him
asking them to dig him
up so we could put him in his
proper place

SKILL

On the way to the funeral I decide I will not be present
I will leave but keep my body there   Instead
I will think about sewing   I will think about the black
Singer shaped like a woman
waiting for me in my mother's house
I will think about the energy of the machine as it makes its
rhythm of stitches   I will think about
cloth   about the jacket I want to make
its back   sleeves   a bodice with darts
a simple collar — how pieces become a
whole   how the thinnest thread
holds   how seams last
if you're careful

SOUNDVIEW

A LOT

Behind the sign that reads   DEAD END
the lot begins   We explore
what's been thrown away
garbage we
refine   bottlecaps become
   crickets   bits of tin foil   Tiffany
diamonds

In tall grass
we hide from each other
pick our teeth with reeds plucked as we
crouch   We slit the shafts with our thumbnails
   milk beads and
        oozes
We sniff and rub 'til it
sticks

Cans and broken
glass   We inscribe our names in the dirt with a
jagged edge   then smooth through with the
edge of a sneaker   a palm dusted on a
cuff

We squat on the Big Rock and
watch the river   my sister's
breath on my ear as she
lifts my braid and

        threads through a
supple weed   appearing and
        disappearing in the
black like an
                              emerald
        ribbon

GLO

The fireflies are out

All the kids have mayonnaise or
jelly jars   nail holes in the lids   We hunt down the
milliseconds of light   but it's
mostly play   almost every jar is
empty

Upstairs
my mother's on the phone
a new beau whispering
      Glo this *Glo* that   as if   she
were a firefly whose warm light he could
capture   the nickname a
      caress

And her beauty so
formal really   unabbreviated
the total inflection of
Gloria   glorious as the evening air we
race through
      life all around us

MIDSUMMER NIGHT

We sit in the steamy dark   close to the
tv   yoga-style   its blue-gray light   the
chiaroscuro of the room
We laugh at
everything   young laughter
for its own
sake

The rug is itchy
against our thighs   sometimes we lie down
press our toes to the screen
its static pop on our
socks

Behind us on the couch   our mother
stretches   cool as a sphinx
    her crimson toenails
miniature taillights   Each time we laugh
she drags on her cigarette
its topaz tip   the distant
signal
of a lighthouse

Beauty Is

My mother as she was   a black

Odalisque   draped in the sheets of her unmade bed
her perfectly shaped legs tucked
one under the other   the curve of her throat   her chin
          exquisitely proportioned   the sculpted
mound of her belly   the mid-calf mole
long as a
     pussywillow

Her breath on the
bathroom mirror as she'd
prepare to go out   accenting eyes already
          perfect
with kohl   outlining lips the color of
grapes at their peak   stepping into a dress that revealed
a body   voluptuous
in its
smallest movement   graceful
in each adjustment of
          torso and hips

My mother's beauty
that lived with us like   another member of the family
     intrinsic
and inviolable   palpable

nourishing

JOHNNYCAKE

It's Sunday morning   pots and pans
banging   sun streams in
She yells for us to
get up for   Jesus   but she won't go
so we stay in bed under the covers
fifteen minutes more

               Then we smell
johnnycake   and know she's
invaded the refrigerator and found the jar of
bacon fat   grease in strata like the earth's
crust   collected for weeks
and added it to flour   We grin
     and jump up for
johnnycake   as if it were our
good daddy come to visit

            We race to the kitchen
where Mommy flips it up   the fragrant cake
its cracked white roads
     I watch as
Lorna pours Alaga
syrup into our plates
     and we break off
bits of johnnycake and dunk them
into the pools

REVEILLE

We are girls in Easter best
pale pinks and blues   yellows that
          don't compliment our skin

My sister's yellow hat   flaps in the cool
March wind   ribbons like kite-tails   while I
dimpled with cold   finger the too-tight elastic band
underneath my chin

          Outside we
show off our new
clothes   pressed for the onset of spring
the dissolution of winter   We shyly watch the other girls
and boys   our vaselined faces gleaming in the
raw morning sun   The door of the building
at our backs   the pavement beneath our chilly feet as
unyielding as
          frozen earth   *Listen*

hear the *tap tap tap* of our new
shoes   black patent leather   with straps and
silver taps
     on the toes

Patent Leather

Spring   is a patent leather season   We buy
new shoes   new pocketbooks   big-girl
pocketbooks
    white black beige   moire linings
We love these pocketbooks   open   close
close   open   gold halves
we press together   *click*   no
    cthuck   almost no sound

In here we place our new
gloves   then take them out
put them in   nestle them   We prance around the
room   our arms crooked like
    tree branches   our palms
smell like patent leather
and that shine   *Touch me!*

We wipe off our fingerprints   breathing on the
mirror leather   our mouths gaping like
    hungry birds

JACKS

A rainy Thursday   we play
jacks

pouring them from their pouch
heavy silver stars that
tink   We scoop them
bouncing the ball against the floor
waxed and
gleaming
     onesies   *twosies*   *threesies*
We throw them wide   a
cascade   or bunch them
a huddle to pluck
        You can't win
if you leave one
behind
      and I cry when I lose
too much   and Lorna smiles
because she knows she is

better

Mrs. Velasquez

Each day when we come
home from school   Mrs. Velasquez cracks her door
and out bounces   Pippa's bark
    like a ball

While I look for my key   we smell Puerto Rico
on high heat

If Lorna is mad
     and yanks my arm
Mrs. Velasquez
    stomps into the hallway
flapping her tropical hem   and shakes her
Spanish on us like
salt and

tells our mother

ORDAINED

You didn't ask to come here my mother sighs
    You didn't ask to be born
as she separates my hair into three
equal pieces to braid
                            I'm locked
between her knees most nights this time
as she plaits my hair   Every now and then she lets
slip
    she would have
        preferred boys
no hair to comb   no hair to
tame
                 We are girls with
    lion hair   Lorna and I
In our dreams we let it
       loose as we rise toward
    Heaven
          which is where   we believe   little girls
come from

AUNT IVY'S

At Aunt Ivy's door   General
licks my face   We've come twenty miles
for this   two and a half
hours   Bronx to Queens (St. Albans)

The boxer wags his
stump *Hello*   Threads of saliva
trail as he paces wondering what to
    make of us

Near the threshold a black and
white photo hangs
    Young Ivy a sprinter   ready to go   Penn Relays 1939
Today
her kiss is
dewy as General's   her pace as
brisk as she escorts us through the kitchen   Uncle
Woodsy twisting to greet us from the second
story   his arthritic
hip raised   his
lips wrapped around a cigar stump
slippery as
    spinach

As the grown-ups chat   Lorna and I
kick up our legs in the
greenhouse   spider

plants   philodendrons   potbound
begonias
     How are Lenny and Myrna? Ivy chirps as she
serves potato salad
        Have you spoken to Leslie? Uncle
Woodsy shagging our hair indulgently and smiling

As late day threads to evening   a behind hand
yawn   crackle of foil as Ivy packs
fried chicken and salad   General curled by his
dish as we leave   two leaden
thumps on the linoleum   his eyes
roving marbles

ICY WAY

You have to have a real thirst
to go down Icy Way

Today the mercury's 103°
gusts off the East River scorch us   we're beans
in a frying pan   All the windows of the un
air-conditioned apartments flung
wide   neighbors hang out
limp as laundry on a line   sweat in the backs of our knees
    Lorna and I
look at each other and decide

It's worth it   start off

across the grass   cut through The Academy Gardens
past the Beach Theatre
down Soundview Avenue
in our pockets coins enough for ices only   no busfare
pick up our cousins
    Leigh and Yvette then one
mile under the elevated trains on Westchester Avenue

At the ices stand we buy
cherry   lemon   orange   tutti-frutti
15¢   We slurp the cold
               don't care
      that   now
blue sky
        is all that
    fills our pockets

THE TENT

Under the tent we've improvised out of
Daddy's army blanket
my sister and I watch Gary Cooper and Marlene Dietrich
fall in love   two hours
in black and white   her question mark
eyebrows   his goofy confusion   We have oranges
from the supermarket   sliced into quarters that
make our mouths   Hollywood smiles
We suck the juice so sweet   pulp
sticks in our teeth   dripping fingers reach
into the bowl 'til they're all
gone   Heads touching on a pillow
air dense as cotton   We yell
    Mom can we have dinner here too?
and she slips under sloppy
joes and corn   only her hands
showing

VISION

Saturday mornings we take turns
going to the supermarket   passing through
the automatic doors of Fedco
      the shopping cart
the list   our mother's handwriting veering
sharply to the right   unambiguous

Lorna goes slow
each aisle spread out before her like a
test paper   each price sticker a
dare   bringing back only what she
has to   the essential
value of each item
calculated before it's placed in the
sack

For me
each aisle is a
cornucopia   I want it
all   and bring back only the
best   loosely interpreting my mother's
calligraphy   digging for the tomato that is
more than a fruit   that is the
epitome of red-orange
exquisitely realized
the brown bags unfolded like flowers
the groceries offered like a
prize

This Old Heart of Mine

Ed Sullivan has come and gone
but all that lovesick summer
sifting through the curtains
still begs for soul music

So we stack 45s and watch the
first one drop
We push the couch out of the way
the chair   the coffee table
where Mommy's discarded
        Vogue
shows us who we'll
never be

We are loose
unwritten pages
Our fingers pop
our heads bop our knees   our
arched behinds   We grind
our hips to the beat
        This Old Heart of Mine

On the corner
Project Man howls for his woman
Maybe she'll let him in
Probably
We know how that goes

First Boy

The first boy I love
is the bald albino   who always wears a hat
gray leather fitted with a sleek
visor to shade his eyes
    his skin a wasted
cream   He hangs
on the fringes of his crowd   the other boys
hot-brown   cinnamon sticks
    bronzed
coffee
      beans   all of them pumped with
youth   jazzed-cocky   funky with layered
sweat and denim   He is silent
shy
       and I
fat with the oils and juices of fifteen
place myself in his way   preen and wait
my long black braid
alive on my back